KU-130-290

The Story of DEFINITIVE STAMPS

RICHARD WEST

EXECUTIVE EDITOR: STAMP MAGAZINE

with

DOUGLAS N. MUIR

CURATOR, PHILATELY: NATIONAL POSTAL MUSEUM

SEFTON LIBRARY SERVICES

Accession No.	Class ✕	Location	
19 42290X	383·2 WES	H	★

Published by Royal Mail, Royal London House,
22-25 Finsbury Square, London, EC2A 1NL.

Text © Richard West and Douglas N. Muir, 1994.

Designed by Silk Pearce.

All rights reserved. No part of this publication may be reproduced, stored in a retrieval system or transmitted in any form or by any means, electronic, mechanical, photocopying, recording or otherwise, without the prior permission of the publishers.

Printed in the United Kingdom by
Raithby, Lawrence & Co Limited, Leicester, LE3 5AY

ISBN 0 946165 04 1

Introduction

Cᴀɴ ʏᴏᴜ ᴛʜɪɴᴋ ᴏғ ᴀɴ ᴇᴠᴇʀʏᴅᴀʏ ᴄᴏᴍᴍᴏᴅɪᴛʏ ᴛʜᴀᴛ
ɪs ᴜsᴇᴅ ɪɴ ᴛʜᴇ ʀᴇɢɪᴏɴ ᴏғ ғᴏᴜʀ ʙɪʟʟɪᴏɴ ᴛɪᴍᴇs ᴇᴠᴇʀʏ
ʏᴇᴀʀ ɪɴ ᴛʜᴇ Uɴɪᴛᴇᴅ Kɪɴɢᴅᴏᴍ ᴀʟᴏɴᴇ; ᴀɴ ɪᴛᴇᴍ ᴛʜᴀᴛ
ʜᴀs ʀᴇᴍᴀɪɴᴇᴅ ᴠɪʀᴛᴜᴀʟʟʏ ᴜɴᴄʜᴀɴɢᴇᴅ ɪɴ ɪᴛs ᴜsᴇ ᴀɴᴅ
ғᴏʀᴍᴀᴛ sɪɴᴄᴇ ɪᴛ ᴡᴀs ɪɴᴠᴇɴᴛᴇᴅ ᴍᴏʀᴇ ᴛʜᴀɴ 150
ʏᴇᴀʀs ᴀɢᴏ? The commodity concerned is the humble postage
stamp, although perhaps not so humble when you realise that
virtually all of the four billion stamps produced each year are
used on mail and some 63 million items of mail are posted in
the UK every working day of the year.

Stamps are not only sold from the 20,000 post offices
nationwide. There are now some 50,000 general retailers selling
stamps as well, available in specially produced booklets. In
addition, many stamps are sold by mail order through Royal
Mail's own British Philatelic Bureau in Edinburgh, which
was established to serve the needs of stamp collectors around
the world.

British stamps are widely acclaimed and avidly collected.
Much of their success can be attributed to the
history and traditions that surround
the postage stamp. It was the UK
that introduced the adhesive postage
stamp to the world in 1840 and,
as a result, stamps from the United
Kingdom are accepted internationally
without the need to include the
name of the country of origin
within their design.

Definitives are those stamps
that remain on sale for as long as
they are needed, often a period
of years, as opposed to Special
Issues, which, by their very
nature, remain on sale from post
offices for just a short while.
The design approach of the

POSTAL DELIVERY

by centre cycle at Horsham,
1882.

first stamps has been largely
retained for the definitive
stamps since adhesive
postage stamps were first
introduced. Included on the
stamps are the portrait of the reigning
monarch, the denomination and, at times,
the words POSTAGE and REVENUE,
although today these are superfluous.

Perhaps even more surprising is the
fact that, despite advances in mail
automation and handling, and changes in
the means of communications, the postage
stamp has remained basically unchanged, and
worldwide it remains the most popular means
of indicating that postage costs have been
prepaid.

Definitive stamps can be divided into three
sections. First, there are the low values. These
are the stamps of standard size that include the
denominations needed for all the basic rates of
postage, such as first- and second-class inland mail, European
(non-EC) mail, worldwide airmail and international postcard
rates. Other values are included for 'make-up' purposes, to
provide the postage required for heavier items.

Second, within the low value category have been added the
non value indicator (NVI) stamps. These are not inscribed with
a particular denomination, but with the service provided, such
as 1st or 2nd for basic weight first-class or second-class inland
mail respectively. The stamps remain valid for the particular
service despite changes that may be levied in the tariff.

Finally, there are the high value definitives. These stamps
are used on heavier items, such as packets and parcels, and they
tend to be larger in size and are often pictorial in nature.

Within the following pages, the story of the highly collected
and collectable definitive stamps will unfold.

THE ONLY POSTMAN
IN NEWCASTLE, *1821,*
before the introduction of
adhesive postage stamps.

POSTMEN COPE *with*
fair weather and foul, as
well as the high tide at
St. Michael's Mount in
Cornwall.

The Birth of the Definitive

THE PENNY BLACK, *the world's first adhesive postage stamp, valid from 6 May 1840 for the prepayment of letters.*

THE TWO PENCE BLUE, *companion to the Penny Black, for heavier letters.*

THE PENNY RED, *which replaced the Penny Black in 1841 because of fears of fraudulent re-use.*

I T'S A STRANGE BUT TRUE FACT THAT AN IDEA DEVELOPED MORE THAN 150 YEARS AGO IS STILL IN USE, VIRTUALLY UNCHANGED, THROUGHOUT THE WORLD TODAY. When Sir Rowland Hill produced his ideas for the reform of the Post Office in the 1830s, he would have little thought that one of the spin-offs would have such a great and lasting significance.

ROWLAND HILL, *father of uniform penny postage - by Mary M Pearson.*

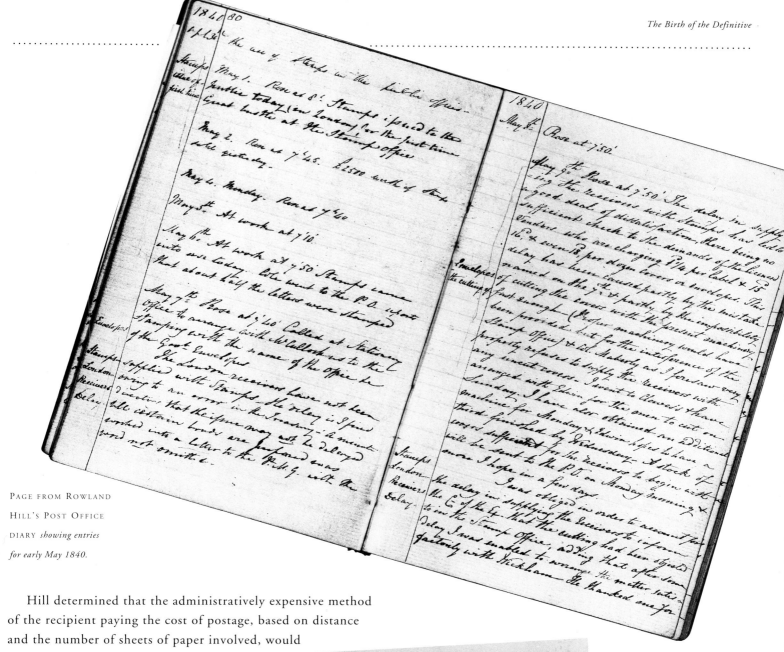

PAGE FROM ROWLAND
HILL'S POST OFFICE
DIARY *showing entries
for early May 1840.*

Hill determined that the administratively expensive method of the recipient paying the cost of postage, based on distance and the number of sheets of paper involved, would be better replaced by the sender paying a cheaper uniform rate based on weight alone.

The concept of a small piece of adhesive paper to indicate that the postage costs had been prepaid was almost an afterthought. Yet the public quickly warmed to this idea when, in May 1840, the famous Penny Black was introduced.

THE PENNY BLACK
USED ON THE FIRST
DAY OF VALIDITY -
6 May 1840.

That very first adhesive postage stamp was so simple in design: the portrait of Queen Victoria with the legends of POSTAGE and ONE PENNY. Simple, yet effective, so that even today the basic postage stamps produced by Royal Mail are of the same size and format, and still bear the royal portrait and denomination alone. These two features are sufficient to tell the world that the item of mail to which the stamp has been affixed comes from the UK and that the postage has been paid.

With the Penny Black, and its contemporary the Two Pence Blue, the definitive stamp was born.

The Penny Black was officially brought into use on 6 May 1840, although it was on sale slightly earlier, so examples are known that were used prior to that date. The Two Pence Blue went on sale on 8 May. One of the major fears expressed by the Post Office at the time was that the stamps might be forged or otherwise misused. Hence the background to the design was complex, and letters were included in the lower corners, with each stamp on a sheet having a different lettering configuration.

In those early days perforations had not yet been introduced, so the stamps had to be cut from the sheet using scissors. Thus, while many millions of Penny Blacks were used – so popular did the use of the postal service become – several million were kept and are available for collectors today, but it is rare to find examples that have been neatly cut from the sheet with clear white margins left around all four sides of the stamp design. Such stamps therefore command a higher price than those with little or no margins.

Perhaps it was their novelty that persuaded the Victorians to retain these new stamps. But whatever the reason, the idea of collecting quickly developed and definitives have remained a fascinating subject for the collector.

The launch of the world's first adhesive postage stamps did spark a surprising level of activity, resulting in a vast array of definitives bearing the portrait of Victoria. The first major change saw the penny stamp transformed from black to

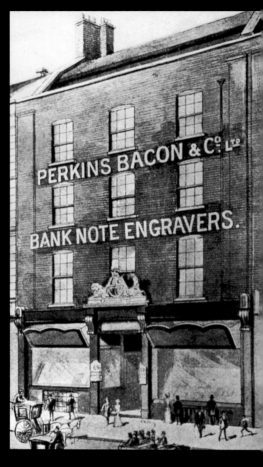

PREMISES OF THE PRINTERS, *Perkins, Bacon & Petch, in Fleet Street.*

Security from forgery or re-use has always been a prime consideration in the design and production of definitive stamps. Although the first stamps, the Penny Black and the Two Pence Blue, were only one method of prepayment of postage at the time, most security measures were concentrated on them.

By combining the considerable talents of Victorian paper

YOU CAN'T FAKE A FACE

makers, engravers and printers one of the finest stamps ever was produced – all in only five months from conception to issue.

The paper incorporated a watermark and the printers, Perkins, Bacon and Petch, added a complicated engine-turned background of their own devising as a background to the design. Rowland Hill also suggested adding different corner letters for each stamp in the sheet of 240. Later this was extended to all four corners so that two uncancelled halves could not be joined together and re-used.

The most important aspect of the Penny Black, however, was its design. Hill thought that is should be 'as beautiful a specimen of fine art as can be obtained' and that there was 'nothing in which minute differences of execution are so readily detected as in a representation of the human face'. He therefore suggested that the head of Queen Victoria be used, based on an embossed die by William Wyon,

perhaps the greatest engraver of the age. Printing was by recess or intaglio from an engraving by the skilled engravers Charles and Frederick Heath.

The remarkably beautiful result has perhaps never been surpassed and it has formed the model for all succeeding definitive stamps not only of the United Kingdom but also for many countries around the world.

THE CITY MEDAL
*by William Wyon, used
as the basis for the head
of Queen Victoria on the
Penny Black.*

PRINTING PRESSES
*used to print the
Penny Black.*

THE ORIGINAL
MASTER DIE
for the Penny Black.

THE INTERIOR
of the General Post
Office, c.1840.

ONE OF THREE

EMBOSSED STAMPS,

the 10d of 1848.

INK TRIALS *for the new*
1d and 2d labels of 1841.

THE GLASGOW PENNY

POSTS, *1838, before*

Hill's reforms.

red-brown in 1841. At first, a red cancellation was used to show that the stamp had served its purpose, but this proved to be removable. As a result, the black stamp was changed to red and the red cancellation to black. The design, however, remained unchanged for some 40 years.

Not only was a multitude of designs introduced during Victoria's reign, differing printing methods were also tested. The first stamps had been line engraved, which causes the design to stand out slightly from the paper in relief; for a short time embossing was used; finally, however, letterpress was adopted, and this gives the smooth surface to the printed face of the stamp we are familiar with today.

While all stamps up to 1s in value were the same size as the Penny Black (and the same size used for the lower value

THE MALTESE CROSS, *the cancellation for the world's first stamps.*

A WEIGHT-COLLECTING LETTER SCALE *by Ratcliff of 1840 - required by the public when payment of letters by weight was introduced.*

THE ORIGINAL
PHOTOGRAVURE
printing press at
Harrison & Sons Ltd,
from 1934.

COUNTING SHEETS
OF STAMPS *in the*
Stamp Section at
Somerset House.

LABELLING REELS OF
STAMPS *ready for*
despatch.

BRITAIN'S SMALLEST

STAMP, *½d for printed*

matter, 1870.

THE SO-CALLED

"JUBILEE" STAMPS

of Queen Victoria were

adapted for those of King

Edward VII.

THE "TYRIAN PLUM"

2d of 1910 which was

never issued because of

the death of The King.

THE "DOWNEY HEAD"

issue of King George V

(left) was replaced by the

"PROFILE HEAD" *(right)*

after a public outcry.

UNADOPTED DESIGN

for a proposed 7d stamp,

by Graham Sutherland.

definitives today), a ½d value issued in 1870 was half the standard size, and it remains the UK's smallest stamp.

In 1887, at the time of Victoria's Golden Jubilee changes were made to the lower value definitives (up to 1s). At the same time, two-colour printing was adopted for several of the values. These same designs were continued into the reign of Edward VII, incorporating a change of portrait. It was Edward VII's reign that produced one of the UK's rarest definitives. A change of design was prepared for the 2d value, but the King's death meant that the stamp was never officially issued. Unused examples of the so-called 2d Tyrian Plum are nevertheless known, and one example has been recorded as being used on a letter sent to the Prince of Wales.

The reign of George V saw much public debate about the design of stamps, because there was general disapproval of the three-quarters portrait used, which had been produced by court photographers W and D Downey. Indeed it was not long before the design was changed to incorporate the more acceptable coinage profile head.

Collectors note that during the early days of George V's reign many of the stamps were printed by either Harrison & Sons or Somerset House. However, 1934 saw a major change, one that has set the basic pattern ever since. From that time (to 1993 when Joh. Enschedé obtained the low value contract) the majority of the lower value definitives have been printed by Harrison & Sons using the photogravure process. Photogravure has proved to be an excellent method for printing definitives because the printing cylinders are long-lasting and thus able to cope with the millions of stamps required every day.

While Edward VIII was never crowned, he was monarch until his abdication on 11 December 1936, and four definitive stamps were issued in September 1936 featuring his portrait. The design was classically simple and, despite the brevity of his reign, the stamps are still relatively common.

THE SIMPLICITY OF EDWARD VIII

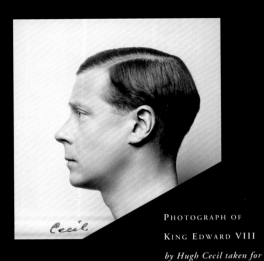

PHOTOGRAPH OF
KING EDWARD VIII
by Hugh Cecil taken for
use on the stamps.

ESSAYS BY HARRISONS
showing King Edward VIII
in the uniform of the
Seaforth Highlanders.

When the stamps of Edward VIII were issued in September 1936 there was considerable surprise at the simplicity of their design. The lack of decoration and the use of a photograph for the first time made a great change from the solid, rather fussy stamps of George V. This change was quite intentional on the part of The King, who wanted to emphasise the differences between himself and his father.

After some initial editorial praise there then ensued a battle royal between artists in the letters pages of The Times, a controversy that itself became news in other papers, and in other countries. The opening shots were from the designer and typographer Eric Gill, who wrote that the stamps marked a bold step in the right direction. Although minor points of detail were to be criticised the photograph was good 'and its reproduction is an admirable example of mechanical expertise'. The lettering was plain and of the right kind and the crown indicated governmental authority. The Post Office was to be congratulated for

ESSAYS OF THE SIMPLE
DESIGN *chosen by the King*
and issued in September
1936.

'releasing us from the banalities of imitation hand-engraving and stupid ornamentation'.

This provoked Edmund Dulac, whose own design had been rejected for the issue, and he replied describing Gill's ideas as confused. 'The new stamps by their simplicity may, in principle, be an improvement on the old ones, but in principle only. One can argue that the elements chosen: King's head, crown, denomination, and lettering are sufficient. An egg, some oil, vinegar, salt and pepper are sufficient elements for an excellent mayonnaise in the hands of a good cook. In the hands of a bad one they can be a mess.' He went on to criticise the head for lack of retouching and that it was not a good likeness; the lettering was commonplace and the composition ill-balanced and empty. The only good piece of design was the watermark.

Gill immediately responded. His argument was that the design was functional. 'A postage stamp is primarily a symbolic device, not a picture.' It had to be produced by the million and the job of a designer was a strictly functional one. Dulac retorted that Gill was insisting on 'the interdependence of three elements that really have only a very slight relationship

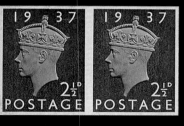

ESSAYS BY ERIC GILL
for a proposed Coronation
issue, never released because
of the King's abdication.

to one another:
machine production,
functionalism, and good
design. In no case is the
functional quality of an
object dependent on
machinery.' Although
functional, a design
may be good or bad.

The argument raged
into October and
spread to the
Manchester Guardian.
Various personalities
in the arts, such as
William Rothenstein,
Frank Pick and Charles
Wheeler, also took part
and it was reported as
far afield as America.
Certainly, the design
caused a considerable
stir and made people
question their accepted
wisdom in design terms.

Some of the criticisms
were undoubtedly
justified - the poor
drawing of the crown,

for example, and the
almost guillotined
appearance of the
head. But not enough
emphasis was placed on
the design being in part
a function of the
printing process,
photogravure. In many
ways, it was the logical
conclusion of a process
that was good for
reproducing tonal
qualities yet poor in
resolving line detail.

It is amusing to note
that the protagonists,
Gill and Dulac, worked
together, apparently
harmoniously, on
stamps for the
succeeding reign, in
which George VI
deliberately returned
to the decorative
symbolism of his father,
rejecting the simplicity
associated with his
brother who had
abdicated.

GEORGE V, LOW
VALUE DEFINITIVES
designed by Edmund
Dulac (head) and Eric
Gill (frames), 1937 - 51.

The simple approach to definitive design was embellished in the reign of George VI, a reign, however, that was to suffer from wartime restrictions. The idea was even considered that the stamp size should be halved in order to economise on paper usage. While this expedient was not adopted, certain stamp colours for a time were made lighter because various inks were no longer available. Further changes of colour can be noted during George VI's reign as part of an international agreement that sought to standardise colours for stamps performing specified functions, such as the basic inland letter rate.

ESSAYS OF SMALLER
STAMPS *proposed to save*
materials during wartime
restrictions, 1943.

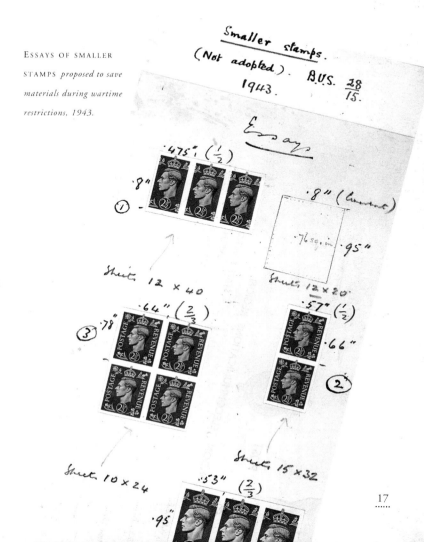

6 February 1952 saw the dawning of the new Elizabethan age, and as the need arose new definitives were gradually introduced featuring the portrait of Elizabeth II from the Dorothy Wilding Studio. Repeating the theme that had been introduced in the previous reign, the designs included the floral emblems of England, Scotland, Wales and Northern Ireland. These 'Wilding' definitives again offer scope for study, mainly because three different watermarks were incorporated into the paper over the years.

The effects of postal mechanisation were also to have an impact, and certain values were experimentally produced with black lines of graphite incorporated on the gummed side of the stamp (in 1957); this technique was subsequently replaced by almost invisible bands of phosphor applied to the face of stamps (in 1959) and phosphor was later incorporated into the coating of the stamp paper. Phosphor is still used on UK stamps today to assist with the automatic sorting and cancelling of mail.

The Wilding design remained in use for some 15 years, until it was replaced in 1967 by what is universally acclaimed to be a masterpiece of stamp design.

DESIGNS USING THE
DOROTHY WILDING
PORTRAIT *of Queen*
Elizabeth II, 1952-1967.

RETOUCHING THE
NEGATIVE *of the*
"Wilding" six pence
stamp, before making the
multi-positive, from
which the printing plate
was produced.

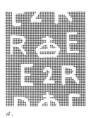  

a.   b.   c.

WATERMARKS USED
ON WILDING
DEFINITIVES:
a. Tudor crown
b. St. Edward's crown
c. Multiple crowns
Multiple crowns were
introduced in 1958 with
the issue of Scottish
"regionals" to avoid E 2 R.

The High Values

While for the majority of users the lower value definitives will prove sufficient, there are many needs for high value stamps. While at first stamps were simply inscribed POSTAGE, later the words AND

THE £5 ORANGE OF
QUEEN VICTORIA,
the highest value postage
stamp for almost 100
years, 1882.

REVENUE were added, since these receipts for payment extended further than just the prepayment of postage.

The higher value definitives have always been regarded as special, their design and printing reflecting their importance. They have also always adopted a larger format. The first higher value – a 5s stamp – was issued in 1867. This was quickly followed by 10s, £1 and, perhaps surprisingly, £5 values. Due to its magnificent design, the £5 stamp is highly regarded by collectors. It remained current for many years, well beyond the end of the reign of Queen Victoria, and there was not a new £5 definitive until 1977.

The addition of a 2s 6d definitive came about in 1883, and this was quickly followed by design changes to the 5s, 10s and £1 values. These four designs, except for a change of

THE £1 OF KING
EDWARD VII,
1902.

A KING GEORGE V
high value in the famous
"Seahorse" design, 1913.

THE FIRST SET OF
HIGH VALUES OF KING
GEORGE VI, *1939-48.*

THE SECOND SET,
released at the time of the
Festival of Britain 1951.

THE FIRST HIGH VALUES
OF QUEEN ELIZABETH II
showing castles, 1955.

portrait, were continued into the reign of Edward VII.

The reign of George V saw a design for the high values that most collectors still hold in high regard. The design is known by collectors as the 'Seahorse', and features Britannia. The four values – 2s 6d, 5s, 10s and £1 – were initially printed by Waterlow Bros and Layton, but subsequently both De La Rue and Co and Bradbury Wilkinson and Co Ltd also printed the three lower values, and collectors are able to distinguish the work of these three printers. Despite the fact that various printing methods were used for the lower value definitives, from 1913 right through to 1977 recess printing alone was used for the higher value definitives.

Two distinct series of high values were used during the reign of George VI. In 1939 the 2s 6d and 5s denominations were issued in a design featuring the Royal coat of arms and, in the same year, these were joined by a 10s value in a floral emblems design. This latter design was also used for the £1 value in 1948.

In 1951 a complete change was made to the design of all four high values, and a more pictorial approach was adopted. Thus the 2s 6d stamp depicted HMS *Victory*, while the 5s featured the White Cliffs of Dover. St George and the Dragon featured on the 10s, and the Royal coat of arms was seen on the £1 stamp. The pictorial approach was retained for the reign of Elizabeth II, and designs featuring UK castles were introduced in 1955. The castles depicted were Carrickfergus (Northern Ireland) on the 2s 6d stamp; Caernarfon (Wales) on the 5s; Edinburgh (Scotland) on the 10s; and Windsor (England) on the £1 stamp. During the life of these designs, it was again necessary to involve the same three printers in their production – Waterlow & Sons Ltd (formerly Waterlow Bros & Layton), De La Rue and Co, and Bradbury Wilkinson and Co Ltd.

The Castle designs remained in use until 1969 when it was felt that the design of the high values should complement that of the lower values.

ENGRAVING THE MASTER PLATE *for one of the 1955 high value stamps.*

MAKING THE PRINTING PLATE *from the hardened transfer roller.*

The Time for Change

ALMOST FROM THE TIME THE NEW STAMPS FOR THE REIGN OF ELIZABETH II APPEARED THERE WERE CALLS FOR CHANGES TO THE DEFINITIVE DESIGNS. There was a reaction against the symbolic approach that had for so long typified United Kingdom stamp design, coupled with a realisation of the power of the postage stamp, exploited fully by Anthony Wedgwood Benn during his time as Postmaster General.

Many of the pleas were for pictorial definitives: some advocates went as far as having their own proposed designs drawn up for submission. In the event, it was pressure from designers that was to persuade Royal Mail that the situation needed to be re-examined. From 1963 special stamp issues were recognised as a way of proclaiming the heritage of the United Kingdom. Prior to that date new stamp issues had been a rarity: now they were to bring additional variety to the everyday mail in a more colourful and pictorial fashion. It was even recognised that there existed a breed known as stamp collectors, who would want to purchase these new releases – not to use on mail but to keep and enjoy.

Many stamp designers felt that the Royal portrait from the Dorothy Wilding Studio used for the definitives was too restrictive to set against the pictorial nature of the Special Issues. As a result, Royal Mail commissioned both the stamp printers and a number of designers to produce ideas for alternative portraits showing how they might be incorporated into both definitive and Special Issue designs.

One of those approached was Arnold Machin, a sculptor who at the time was working on a new portrait for UK coinage. His ideas for incorporating a new portrait within a revised definitive design, together with suggestions from other designers, were considered by the Stamp Advisory Committee. This body was established to advise Royal Mail on matters relating to the design of postage stamps. Its members are not Royal Mail employees, but representatives of a wide range of public interests, including philately and design.

ARNOLD MACHIN *working on the clay relief of The Queen's head.*

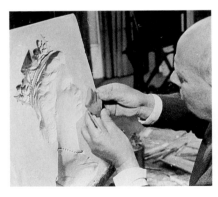

AFTER A CAST HAS BEEN MADE *he checks the detail of the eye by making a clay impression.*

The concept that gained most favour was that of Arnold Machin, who used as his inspiration the classic Penny Black design. Simplicity was the principle he adopted, with just the Royal portrait and the denomination. It was not felt necessary even to include the legend POSTAGE on the design.

Machin produced several sculptures for the portrait, and each was meticulously photographed under varying lighting conditions to achieve the perfect results wanted. The final choice of portrait lay with Her Majesty. In fact, two versions of the portrait were selected, one suitable for placing with a gradated background; the other better suited to a solid background colour.

THE FINISHING TOUCHES *to the head, for the new definitive stamp.*

THE FIRST THREE
MACHIN LOW VALUE
DEFINITIVES *of*
5 June 1967.

The first three values in the new design were issued on 5 June 1967. The Machin definitives had been born.

The unanimous reaction was one of praise. What had been created was a design that had both simplicity and dignity – a beauty that many compared with the Penny Black. The three values that launched the series were the 4d, 1s and 1s 9d. The colour of the 4d was olive brown sepia, selected at the request of Her Majesty. Regrettably this dark colour created difficulties with the signal given by the phosphor bands, and thus proved less effective with the automatic letter facing equipment. Consequently the colour of this stamp was changed to scarlet. The 1s value used the pale background approach, the colour chosen being violet. The 1s 9d saw a return to definitives printed in more than one colour for the first time since the reign of King Edward VII: this stamp was printed in tangerine orange and olive brown. Gradually all the lower value denominations became available in the Machin design.

With such a striking design, the view was taken that it should be used throughout the definitive range. Thus, while previously the higher values had had their own distinctive designs, now the high values would also feature just the Machin portrait and denomination, in the same format as that used for the lower values only larger.

THE MACHIN DESIGN
engraved for the pre-
decimal high values.

Two lines of shading in
the hair.

BROMIDE OF THE
MACHIN HEAD
as used for stamps with
solid backgrounds.

Missing pearl in necklace.

One line of shading in
the hair.

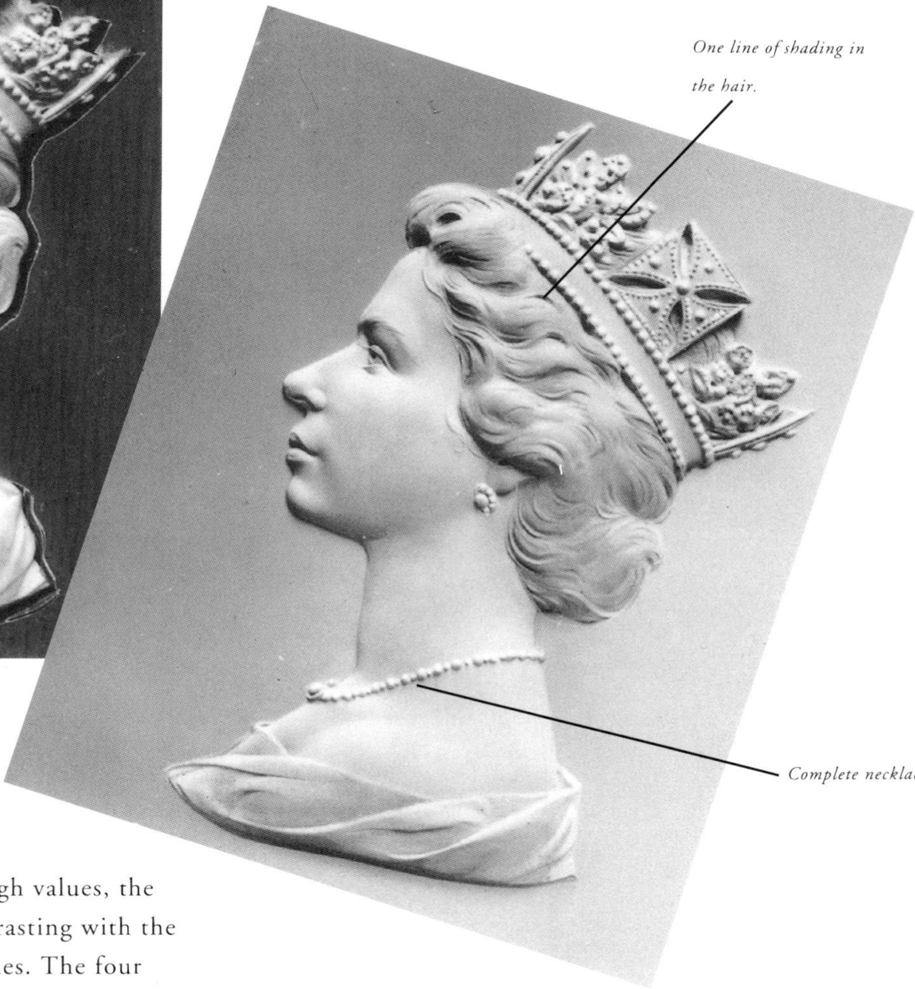

Complete necklace.

Nevertheless, in keeping with previous high values, the recess method of printing was retained, contrasting with the photogravure method used for the lower values. The four stamps comprising the higher values were 2s 6d, 5s, 10s and £1 and they were first issued in March 1969 in sheets of 40 stamps.

Their life was to be short, however, for just over a year later they were superseded by revised denominations in anticipation of the introduction of decimal currency.

BROMIDE OF THE
MACHIN HEAD
as used for stamps
with graduated tone
backgrounds.

THE GENESIS OF THE MACHIN DESIGN

In 1965 the then Postmaster General Anthony Wedgwood Benn obtained the Queen's permission to prepare studies for a new definitive series, using a new profile head rather than the three-quarters portrait by Dorothy Wilding dating from 1952. Photographs taken by Lord Snowdon were supplied to selected artists as the basis for their designs, and work was submitted by David Gentleman and Arnold Machin among others.

Machin based his work on the drawings he had done of the Queen's head for the new coinage, as well as on the Penny Black. His approach was preferred and he proceeded to produce a plaster cast of the Queen's head that was similar to his coin design but facing the other way. From this, photographs were taken and essays prepared by the printers, Harrison & Sons, with the head set in various frames and with different regional symbols.

The first essays were produced in April 1966

but Machin was not satisfied with the result and the cast was rephotographed by John Vickers and further essays produced. All these were based ultimately on the Snowdon photographs but the desired simplicity had not been achieved.

An alternative to the sculptured approach of Machin was required and so John Hedgecoe took a series of photographs of the Queen in June 1966, and David Gentleman worked on these to provide a photographic alternative. The essays were produced by Harrison & Sons towards the end of the year.

By this time Machin had simplified his sculpture. His second plaster cast was a smaller version showing only the Queen's head and neck. She was wearing a tiara as in the previous cast. Essays were prepared from this cast on 19 October with plain background colours and only the value as legend. Gone were the words POSTAGE and

REVENUE as well as any superfluous decoration. When these were shown to members of the Stamp Advisory Committee (with the Hedgecoe photograph essays) they were regarded as a great improvement. The Committee suggested that the tiara be replaced by the diadem as on the Wilding definitives. Machin immediately

sculpted a new mould and formed a head recognisably similar to that finally used. Various photographs were taken under different lighting conditions and essays were printed on 31 October 1966, again with plain backgrounds.

When shown the essays, the Queen expressed a preference

PRELIMINARY SKETCHES *by Arnold Machin.*

for a corsage or clothing around the bust, so Machin added this and translated it into a new sculpture that he photographed many times until he was satisfied with the modelling and lighting. The first essays with the final Machin cast were printed in December and subsequently a large number produced to establish the colours that should be used on the finished stamps.

Two plaster casts were produced by Machin with the corsage. One was used to produce stamps with a graduated background and the other for stamps with a solid background. The Queen herself chose the colour of the standard inland rate - an olive brown sepia. Shortly after its introduction, however, it had to be changed because the dark colour, consciously chosen to imitate that of the Penny Black, was too strong for the phosphor signal needed for the automatic cancelling machinery.

The stamp's classic simplicity harks back to the Penny Black, and the design is still in use today, some 27 years after its introduction.

THE FIRST MACHIN ESSAYS *with regional symbols April/May 1966.*

THE SECOND SIMPLIFIED MACHIN DESIGN *(left) preferred to the essay based on the photograph by Hedgecoe (right) October 1966.*

THE THIRD MACHIN DESIGN *showing the development of the corsage. Essays of December 1966.*

ESSAYS OF THE FINAL DESIGN, *the 4d value being issued with the value to the left. March 1967.*

ARNOLD MACHIN VIEWS THE FINISHED STAMPS *as they come off the printing press.*

ROYAL MAIL
HIGH VALUE
DEFINITIVE
STAMPS

CARRICKFERGUS CASTLE   CAERNARFON

£1   £1.50

£1   £1.50   £2   £5
CAERNARFON CASTLE   EDINBURGH CASTLE   WINDSOR CASTLE

FERGUS

High Value Definitive Stamp
Royal Mail First Day Cover

Pounds

£10

MAIL
UE
IVE
S

Royal Mail High Value Definitive Stamp

TENPOUNDSTENPOUNDSTEN

£10

37ᵖ   34ᵖ   29ᵖ   20ᵖ   15ᵖ

FIRST DAY OF ISSUE 10 JAN 1990

THE COLLECTION
TOLKIEN'S

SELF-ADHESIVE STAMPS

1ST

1ST

20
First
Class

Royal Mail

Self-adhesive stamps.
No need to lick.
Just bend, peel and stick.

Printed by Walsall Security
Printers Limited

1840   1990

PENNY BLACK
ANNIVERSARY STAMPS
ROYAL MAIL FIRST DAY COVER

Mrs J Rob
200 Manor.
ILKEST
Derbys
DE7 4

Mrs J Rob
200 Manor.
ILKESTON
Derbyshire
DE7 4AB

SELF-ADHESIVE STAMPS

FIRST DAY OF ISSUE BRITISH

DEFINITIVE STAMPS CAN BE
COLLECTED *in a wide range of
attractive forms, from first day
covers to 'prestige' stamp books.*

SELF-ADHESIVE
DEFINITIVE STAMPS

UNADOPTED COLOURS
FOR THE DECIMAL
STAMPS *from the*
Cambridge trials.

THE COLOURS OF THE
STAMPS *as issued after*
the Cambridge trials,
with values shown in
manuscript.

Decimalisation

Decimal currency came to the United Kingdom on 15 February 1971: the public had been gradually introduced to the idea that the pound would in future comprise 100 new pence as opposed to the former 240 old pence. As part of this education process, on 17 June 1970 Royal Mail issued revised high values in the denominations of 10p, 20p and 50p (equivalent to 2s, 4s and 10s). The design was that which had been introduced for the high values the previous year, featuring just the Machin portrait with the denomination, and still printed by the recess process. Since the pound remained the basic unit of currency, there was no need to change this particular stamp's design, but it was re-issued in a changed sheet format comprising 100 stamps. Later, in 1972, the typeface used for £1 denomination was changed to provide uniformity with the rest of the decimal series.

On Decimalisation Day, all the lower value definitives appeared in decimal currency, from ½p to 9p. At that time the cost of sending a letter by first-class post was 3p, and by second-class post 2½p. As with the previous Machin series, a variety of styles was used: some values, such as the 1p and 2p, used a dark-coloured background; others, such as the ½p and 2½p, used a light-coloured background. One value, the 9p, was printed in two colours.

Before the decimal definitives were released one of the difficulties that had been encountered with the Machin series was addressed. Using the same basic design throughout the range meant that it was by colour that the various denominations would be distinguished. Prior to decimalisation it had been found that the olive brown sepia originally selected for the 4d value presented certain operational problems. Just over a year after the launch of the Machin designs a two-tier postal system was introduced (in September 1968), with the basic rates being 4d or 5d depending on the service required. The 5d had been a Stewart blue, which under certain lighting conditions was not sufficiently distinguishable from the olive brown sepia of the 4d value.

FIRST ISSUE
decimal coins.

As a result much time was spent in considering the best range of colours, bearing in mind certain criteria. First, the colours of the stamps had to be easily distinguishable, particularly under artificial light and in relation to the denominations most widely used. In this respect, consideration had also to be given to future tariff changes. As it happened, this was a wise consideration, since the early 1970s witnessed a period of high inflation that necessitated a revision of tariffs at least once a year.

Royal Mail was by now making increased use of mechanical sorting, and it was found that stamps of certain colours provided a better signal with such equipment. The final, but not least, consideration was the aesthetics of any colour chosen. With such a striking design it was essential that the colours fully complement the Machin sculpture.

When the decimal series was in the planning stage it was realised that there would be a need for 14 low values, and thus the same number of colours or shades. A possible 40 colours were selected, and the first task was to have these tested by engineers in order to assess their performance with mechanical sorting equipment. The result was that 25 colours were left from which stamp colours could be selected. Further examination took place at Cambridge University to test whether these 25 colours were easily distinguishable visually. Each of the colours was arranged in pairs – with itself and with each of the remaining 24 colours. Two teams, one comprising housewives and the other postmen, were then invited to state whether each pair was the same or different. From this, 14 colours were selected that could be readily distinguished both visually and by the mechanical sorting equipment.

Few people could have anticipated the levels of inflation that were to be witnessed over the years immediately following decimalisation. It quickly became apparent that the 10p, 20p and 50p values could no longer be described as 'high' and, therefore, first the 10p, and later the 20p and 50p,

changed to the smaller, low value format. At first the 10p, as the 9p, was printed in two colours, but increased usage meant that such two-colour printing was not justified, and so both values changed to single-colour printing.

In the years since decimal currency was introduced, not only has the range of denominations expanded considerably, but also the use made of the postal system has significantly increased, resulting in a greater demand for stamps. While the vast majority of the millions of stamps required every day are printed by photogravure and were by Harrison & Sons, it has now been found necessary to use other security stamp printers, and also to use the lithographic printing process.

The progress made in stamp printing has meant that the quality of the stamps produced lithographically is now more able to match those stamps printed by photogravure. However, the nature of the printing cylinders means that photogravure can cope with far larger print runs before they wear out and have to be changed. Nevertheless, over the years good use has been made of the lithographic skills of John Waddington Security Print Ltd, The House of Questa and Walsall Security Printers Ltd, and the services of Joh. Enschedé en Zonen in The Netherlands are now also used for photogravure printing.

Over the years there have been suggestions of a change from the Machin design, but it proved difficult to break with this classic and highly considered design. However, a definitive that enjoys such a long life, and that is in use during a period of high inflation when postal rates needed to be revised at least once, and sometimes twice, a year, can suffer from the necessities of compromise.

While a review of the range of low value definitives all the way through from the lowest – ½p – to the highest – 75p so far – provides an impressive array of colours, not all, unfortunately, may be considered entirely suited to the design. Understandably some colours would be repeated. It would be impossible to find a 'new' colour every time a stamp

THE PRINTING PROCESSES

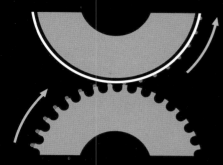 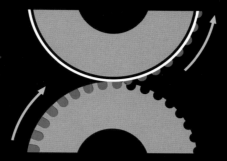 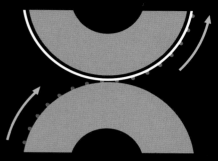

Letterpress, or relief printing, is the oldest of the major printing methods. The ink is transferred directly from the raised surface of the printing plate onto the paper by means of pressure.

When the Gravure process is used the ink is held in recessed cells etched into the surface of the printing cylinder. When printed under pressure the paper draws the ink out of the etched areas.

With offset lithography the ink adheres to the greasy image area on the, otherwise damp, flat surface of the printing plate. It is transferred via a rubber blanket on to the paper.

RETOUCHING *a photogravure cylinder.*

THE JUMELLE PHOTOGRAVURE *printing press at Harrison & Sons Ltd.*

THE FIRST ENGRAVED
DECIMAL HIGH
VALUES *(with the
revised £1 sign).*

appeared in a denomination not previously used. Equally, over
the years certain denominations, made temporarily redundant
because they did not correspond to a current postal rate, would
have to be brought back into use again. While the value
printed on the stamp may be unchanged, the rate it prepaid
may have indeed altered, and thus its colour would need to be
different. As a result, stamps of the same denomination in a
collection may appear in different colours.

HIGH VALUE *printed
gravure, 1977.*

By the mid 1980s it was felt that the colour compromises
made to the Machin series had seriously affected its appeal.
Arnold Machin's original design had featured a light
portrait against a dark background, but this concept had
been lost almost from the outset. Nevertheless, it was
generally agreed that the design was most effective
when the original principle was adopted. An idea that
was put forward was to use the same colour for a
particular rate (such as the inland first-class rate),
but to alternate between dark and light shades as
tariffs were revised. In general, this principle seemed
to hold good, except when a certain denomination paid a
particular rate before a tariff change, and happened to prepay

a different rate following the change. This would necessitate a colour change – a situation that needs to be avoided since it can lead to confusion.

The problem of rationalising stamp colours was given to Jeffery Matthews, a designer with many years' experience of working with Royal Mail. He developed the idea of using pairs of (light and dark) colours, carefully hand mixing each shade. In this way Matthews was able to ensure that just the right colour was selected, being careful throughout to check the colours under differing lighting conditions to ensure that no confusion could occur. Working closely with Harrison & Sons, the various colours were proofed and several samples taken to ensure consistency.

In the end, 16 strong, distinctive colours were selected, although even this number proved insufficient to meet all requirements, and so a further 16 colours were requested.

For each of the chosen colours, Harrison & Sons produced proof sheets. These are retained so that constant checks can be made to ensure that colour standards are maintained. This is particularly important when stamps are produced by other printers or when other printing processes are used, since it is vital that the colours still match as closely as possible.

Colour quality control became particularly significant during 1993 when it was decided to remove the optical brightening agent that had been incorporated within the surface coating of stamp paper. This agent had been used for many years, and had the effect of making the paper look whiter and brighter. The change came about when it was found that the chemicals used were not helpful to the phosphor signal; they were not particularly friendly to the environment either. Omitting this agent means that stamp paper takes on a creamier appearance, a fact that needs to be compensated for by stringent colour standards.

The work on the colours was not the only involvement Jeffery Matthews has had with the Machin definitives. The original typeface used by Arnold Machin for the

denomination had been perfect before decimalisation, but with the change of currency and the effects of inflation, certain denominations were occupying more space than could happily be accommodated within the stamp without cluttering the design. Matthews therefore devised a slimmer typeface, one that still maintained the classic forms of the original but one that also fitted comfortably within the space.

Over the years the increased range of colours had created some compromises with the original Machin concept, and there had also been difficulties associated with printing high values in recess. Finally these difficulties became insurmountable. There had been a gradual need to revise the concept of high values, since the original 10p, 20p and 50p could no longer be classified as 'high'. As a result, in 1977 the opportunity was taken to review the high value range.

It was decided that these should, like the low values, be printed photogravure by Harrison & Sons, thereby giving conformity to the entire definitive range. A larger, vertical format was adopted, allowing for a larger version of the Machin portrait, with the denomination being slightly repositioned compared with the low values. It was appropriate that the denominations should now be £1, £2 and £5 – the first time a £2 stamp had been issued, and the first £5 since that issued in the reign of Queen Victoria. Each value was printed in two colours.

In 1983 it was felt that a single stamp should be issued to prepay the basic parcel rate, so that users would not have to affix several stamps to make up the required value. As postal rates were revised each year from 1983 to 1987 inclusive, a new 'parcel' rate stamp was issued, in denominations of £1.30, £1.33, £1.41, £1.50 and £1.60 respectively. In each case, the design was that adopted for the high values in 1977.

Since the Machin design remains in use, some might believe the story has come to an end. However, wider availability of stamps and the need to be alert to security problems means that such is far from the case.

150 Years on

THE PENNY BLACK
ANNIVERSARY
DEFINITIVE *by*
Jeffery Matthews in
the colour of the Two
Pence Blue.

MAIL COACH
EXCHANGING MAILS
at dawn with a
postmaster along the
way, c. 1840.

WHEN ROYAL MAIL ANNOUNCED THE SPECIAL STAMP PROGRAMME FOR 1990, NO MENTION WAS MADE OF THE 150TH ANNIVERSARY OF THE PENNY BLACK. A number of collectors were more than surprised by this omission. The reality was that such an important anniversary was to be commemorated in an unusual and special way.

It was decided that the definitives used for prepayment of the basic inland and overseas services (15p, 20p, 29p, 34p and 37p) appear in a new design during 1990 to mark the occasion. Jeffery Matthews was given the task of designing a new definitive, which would still retain the classical lines of the Machin series yet provide the user with a clear reminder of the Penny Black.

It was fortunate that the Penny Black and Machin designs had been regarded as being in the same genre. By taking the portrait of Victoria, as used for the Penny Black, and the Machin portrait of Elizabeth II, and slightly overlapping the two, Matthews was able to combine the two elements of his brief in a single design.

The five values were released on 10 January 1990, itself a significant anniversary. Sir Rowland

TODAY, ROYAL MAIL
SKYNET *planes airlift*
post throughout the UK
each night.

Hill's reform of the Post Office envisaged a simple rate for the prepayment of postage to be determined by the weight of the item. Hill considered that this basic rate should be one penny, but as an interim measure, a uniform fourpenny rate was introduced in 1839. The uniform penny rate came into being on 10 January 1840, for the prepayment of which the adhesive postage stamp was introduced in May 1840. The Penny Black definitives remained in use for most of 1990, until tariffs were revised in September of that year.

For the year from October 1989 the 15p second-class definitive was printed in blue, and the 20p first-class in black, to emulate the Two Pence Blue and Penny Black. A facsimile Penny Black appeared in the miniature sheet marking the international stamp exhibition, Stamp World London 90, held in London between 3 and 13 May, 1990. Here the main design was based on that of the George V 'Seahorse' high values with an impression of the Penny Black and the 20p anniversary definitive added. The Penny Black derived from the original die held in the National Postal Museum.

While the Penny Black on the miniature sheet was printed by the recess process, the 20p anniversary definitive also included was printed by photogravure. This 20p value was separately perforated within the miniature sheet.

This special item was sold at £1, the surcharge helping to offset the cost of staging the international stamp exhibition and the part that Royal Mail played at the event, particularly in encouraging the hobby of stamp collecting among the young.

STAMP WORLD
LONDON 90
MINIATURE SHEET
featuring the Seahorse design and incorporating a gravure Anniversary definitive.

Cable to CANADA, etc.., "via IMPERIAL."

Book of STAMPS
10 @ 1½d. 6 @ 1d.
6 @ ½d.
2/-
49

BUY
PUNCH
"THE FOREMOST HUMOROUS JOURNAL IN THE WORLD."

SEND A GREETINGS TELEGRAM
14
GPO STAMPS 2/6
6 at 2½d · 6 at 2d · 6 at ½d

For telling how & why & when use Stephens' Ink in a Stephens' Pen

6/-

£1.15
Royal Mail Stamps
Ten at 11½p

£1.46
Royal Mail Stamps
6 at 16p
First Class
4 at 12½p
Second Class

Postal History 8
Seahorse High Values

10/-
TEN SHILLINGS
POSTAGE

1850-1860
Fourth of six illustrations by Eric Stemp on nineteenth century women's costume. Printed by Harrison & Sons Limited.

£1.55
Royal Mail Stamps

GREETINGS for CHRISTMAS 1980
Royal Mail Stamps
£2.20
Ten at 10p
Ten at 12p

Pantomimes drawn by Barbara Brown

£1
Royal Mail Stamps
Four at 25p

Christmas Special Offer
30p off
Royal Mail Stamps

Winston Churchill (1874 – 1965)
Third in a series on twentieth-century prime ministers illustrated by Harry Brockway. Printed by Walsall Security Printers Limited.

50p
Royal Mail Stamps
Three at 12½p
Four at 3p
One at ½p

on Rare Farm Animals (supported by The Rare Breeds Survival Trust

A FEW OF THE MANY definitive stamp book covers that have been produced over the years

Serving The Public

POSTMASTER'S NOTICE
OF ISSUE *of stamp*
booklets, 1904.

THE VAST MAJORITY OF STAMPS ARE PURCHASED OVER THE POST OFFICE COUNTER AND SO THEY ARE PRODUCED IN LARGE SHEETS. However, this may not always be the most convenient way for the customer to purchase stamps.

Today vending machines do not dispense single stamps, only booklets, but at one time the most commonly used definitives could be purchased singly or in strips from machines strategically positioned often outside post offices. For For a period in the early years of the Machin definitives, certain machines dispensed a strip of stamps in various denominations covering a variety of postal rates.

For many users, however, the stamp booklet has proved to be the most handy way of purchasing stamps. Royal Mail has always been careful in the production of these booklets, using specially printed sheets with an adequate binding margin.

The first official stamp booklet appeared in 1904 and in the early years a supplement of ½d was made. This extra charge did not last long, however, and by the reign of George V customers were paying just the face value of the stamps within the booklet. For many years stamp booklets had rather perfunctory covers, although in 1917 commercial advertising was allowed on the front covers. Later covers reverted to providing just the price and stamp content of the booklet, although commercial advertising still appeared on the interleaves between the stamp panes. Indeed, on occasions advertising appeared on a label printed within the panes of stamps. Generally speaking, the booklet covers, interleaves and panes of stamps were held together by stitching.

ISSUE OF BOOK OF POSTAGE STAMP

BOOKS containing twenty four 1d. Stamps are now on sale at this Office — price 2s. 0½d. each.

The Books are of a convenient size for carrying in the pocket, and information as to the Rates of Postage and other Postal matters is printed on the covers.

By Command

GENERAL POST OFFICE,
15th March, 1904.

STAMP VENDING MACHINE *outside a Post Office, 1936.*

In an attempt to inject new vitality into stamp booklets, pictorial covers were introduced in 1968, and cover designs were changed at regular intervals. This general practice is still in use today, with booklet cover designs being produced in short series with a particular theme.

Another major change took place in 1976: to simplify the production of booklets, the stitched versions were replaced by a booklet in which the stamp pane was affixed within a card cover. Pictorial covers were retained for most of these.

An advantage of this style of booklet is that it can be more easily dispensed by machine. However, clearly such booklets must be sold at a straightforward price – at times, variously 10p, 50p, £1 and £2. To provide stamps that both total the amounts indicated, and that provide for a maximum range of the most commonly used postal rates, booklets often contain panes of stamps of more than one denomination. If you encounter stamps of two different denominations printed joined together, the likelihood is that they have come from such a booklet.

In an effort to encourage the use of stamp booklets, for a time during the 1980s certain discount offers were introduced. By purchasing a booklet, customers made a saving on the normal cost of the stamps. To distinguish such 'discounted' stamps, they were often printed with a letter D on the gummed side. A further use of discounted stamps occurred during the 1980s on stamps for use during the Christmas period. For several years booklets were produced containing a selection of definitive stamps for use on Christmas cards. From 1982 to 1986 inclusive such booklets were sold at a discount rate, and these stamps were distinguished by a 'star' printed on the gummed side. Christmas stamp booklets are still produced each year, but now they contain the special stamps produced to celebrate the Christmas season.

Stamp collectors have always enjoyed a love-hate relationship with booklets. For many years the panes of stamps within booklets had perforations around all edges, but the method of production, by which each booklet is guillotined to size, meant that these perforations were often trimmed or removed. To please collectors, therefore, the outer perforations on certain booklet panes were dispensed with altogether. Many regard an imperforate stamp as a arity – and indeed on the very rare occasions when a stamp misses the perforation process, a collectable error will result. However, if you find a stamp with just one edge without perforations, it is likely to have come from a booklet pane.

Mention should now be made of a stamp booklet development that started in 1969 – that of sponsored booklets, the contents of which would be devoted to a single firm. The booklets were envisaged as being more ambitious than usual, having a larger format and colour illustrations throughout. The selling price would also be higher than normal, but the booklets would contain a wide range of stamps, and their face value would equal the selling price. The first such booklet was devoted to recipes from the Milk Marketing Board, and contained one pound's worth of stamps. Similar booklets devoted to Wedgwood appeared in 1972 and 1980. But it was in 1982 that the idea for these booklets really caught on, and they are now produced annually.

POSTER ADVERTISING

stamp booklets, 1934.

FIRST VICTORIAN *letter box (painted green).*

VICTORIAN *Penfold letter box.*

LETTER BOX *from the reign of George V.*

ELIZABETH II *double aperture letter box.*

ELIZABETH II *rectangular letter boxes.*

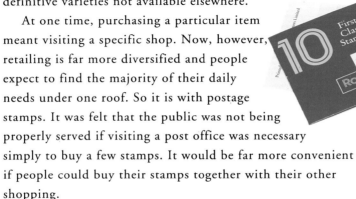

EACH 'PRESTIGE' STAMP
BOOK *focuses on a particular*
subject and includes a special
pane of definitive stamps.

Today such booklets are rightly described as 'Prestige', and instead of being sponsored they tend to focu focus on a particular subject that er is better handled by such a pictorial booklet than with a special issue of stamps. The total face value of the stamps in the booklets is usually equal to the selling price, and normally the contents include a selection of definitive values, although appropriate special or greetings stamps are sometimes included. These booklets often include definitive varieties not available elsewhere.

At one time, purchasing a particular item meant visiting a specific shop. Now, however, retailing is far more diversified and people expect to find the majority of their daily needs under one roof. So it is with postage stamps. It was felt that the public was not being properly served if visiting a post office was necessary simply to buy a few stamps. It would be far more convenient if people could buy their stamps together with their other shopping.

BOOKLET WITH
NON VALUE INDICATOR
definitives stamps

SALE OF STAMP
BOOKLETS *at*
newsagents.

A ROLL OF STAMPS
produced for a vending
machine.

A new range of stamp booklets was developed, intended to be sold not only over post office counters but also through a wide range of retail outlets. These booklets, introduced in 1987, are distinguished by their bright red and yellow covers, and mostly contain either four or ten stamps of the basic first- and second-class inland letter rates. They quickly proved their worth and have become extremely popular with customers.

At first these booklets had a small window in the front cover so that the contents could be seen: as a result, stamp collectors designated them as 'window books'. Today, the window has been replaced by an illustration of the stamp content, but collectors still use the old

BRITAIN'S FIRST
SELF-ADHESIVE STAMP,
available in booklets, 1993.

title together with the newer 'Red' or 'Retail' books.

Encouraging the public to buy their stamps in these booklets posed a potential difficulty at a time of a tariff change. It was unreasonable to expect customers to have to go to a post office to purchase 'make-up' values for any old rate stamps they still had. The solution was to issue stamps that served a particular function rather than had a specific denomination. So stamps were issued, in booklets, bearing the legend 1st or 2nd, designating them for basic first- or second-class letter rates respectively (they are termed NVIs – Non Value Indicators – by Royal Mail). To help commercial users, such first- and second-class stamps have also later been made available in sheets from selected sources.

These stamps still remain in use, and they are always valid for the service stated, irrespective of any tariff changes. While at first such stamps were only accepted on mail within the United Kingdom, they can now be used on mail to many other countries, and their value is taken as the then current first- or second-class rates.

Despite the success already enjoyed by these stamp booklets, there will be considerable additional growth in the variety of sources from which they may be purchased.

Ever aware of the need to serve the public, Royal Mail introduced self-adhesive stamps in 1993, initially on an experimental basis. It is perhaps somewhat ironic that while in general the idea of moistening a piece of paper to affix it seems outdated, it is only in very recent years that the self-adhesive stamp has been developed due to Royal Mail's demand that self-adhesive stamp quality is equal to that of gummed stamps. However, several countries have been experimenting with this type of stamp – with mixed results – and so Royal Mail has decided to offer the public the chance to see if they would prefer not to have to lick their stamps.

The new self-adhesive stamp is included in booklets for sale through post offices and general retailers in the Tyne-Tees television region.

ADVERTISEMENTS

from early stamp books.

"G TYPE" *stamp*

machine, 1969.

Increasing Security

WHILE THE IDEA OF HAVING A DEFINITIVE SERIES THAT WAS UNIFORM IN STYLE FOR BOTH THE LOW AND HIGH VALUES WAS SOUND, IN MANY WAYS IT FAILED TO ATTACH AN AIR OF IMPORTANCE TO THE HIGHER DENOMINATIONS. Imagine the reaction if all currency was in the form of coins, and the use of banknotes was suspended.

Many regarded the design of Royal Mail's high values as outstanding, especially the 'Seahorse' designs of 1913 and the 'Castles' introduced in 1955. So the decision was made to create a new series based on the same fine design principles. The theme chosen was again castles, and the subjects were to be based on photographs commissioned from HRH The Duke of York. The recess method of printing would again be used.

The four castles selected were the same as those used in 1955: Carrickfergus Castle (£1), Caernarfon Castle (£1.50), Edinburgh Castle (£2) and Windsor Castle (£5). These four stamps were released on 18 October 1988.

A problem that is posing a potential threat to postal administrations throughout the world is that of stamp forgery. With modern laser colour copying equipment, quite accurate reproductions can be achieved relatively easily and so suitable action needs to be taken. Working on the principle that prevention is better than cure, Royal Mail decided to review its high values.

A number of security measures were built into the high values, the most visually obvious being the use of optically variable ink for the silhouette of the Queen (which varies in colour from gold to green, depending on the angle at which it is viewed), and the inclusion of an elliptically shaped perforation (to replace three of the normal perforation holes) on the left and right of each stamp. These revised high values were released on 24 March 1992: on the previous day, the earlier Castle issue of 1988 was withdrawn from sale.

By 1993 an operational need had arisen for a £10 definitive for international postage and customs dues. Clearly a significant stamp was required, and the result was a stunning

WINDSOR CASTLE *as seen on the 1955 high values.*

WINDSOR CASTLE *as seen on the 1988 high values.*

CAERNARFON CASTLE

THE 1992 HIGH VALUES. *The Queen's head on these stamps is printed in optically variable ink which changes colour from gold to green when viewed at different angles.*

CARRICKFERGUS CASTLE

PHOTOGRAPHS BY THE DUKE OF YORK *were used for 1988 and 1992 high values stamps.*

EDINBURGH CASTLE

WINDSOR CASTLE

THE BRITANNIA
£10 STAMP *with many
security features including
braille dots, 1993.*

PRINTING THE £10
STAMP *showing the
fluorescent ink glowing
under the ultraviolet
light.*

EXAMINING *one of
the film separations.*

design reflecting the brilliance of the George V 'Seahorses'.
This magnificent stamp, twice the size of the other high values,
bears the design of Britannia, and it is superbly printed using
the lithography process.

To assist those with poor eyesight, the stamps include the
denomination £10 in braille, something that also doubles as a
security measure. In addition the stamps have a wide range of
security features, including a silver die-stamped silhouette of
the Queen, coloured threads in the paper and, once again,
elliptical perforations. One of the easiest methods of
preventing the forgery of stamps is to include such elliptical
perforations. As a result they are now found on stamps issued
in booklet and coil form, as well as on all new printings of
definitives in sheets.

LATER 1d REDS *had alternate corner letters so that two halves of different stamps could not be joined and fraudulently re-used.*

LARGE CROWN WATERMARK *as used on some Victorian definitives.*

ELLIPTICAL PERFORATIONS *introduced in 1992.*

PHOTOGRAPHING THE ORIGINAL ARTWORK *for the £10 stamp.*

UNADOPTED DESIGN
FOR SCOTLAND *by*
Stuart Barne, 1958.

UNADOPTED DESIGN
FOR SCOTLAND
DECIMAL STAMPS *by*
Jock Kinneir, 1971.

UNADOPTED DESIGN
FOR SCOTLAND
DECIMAL STAMPS *by*
Jeffery Matthews, 1971.

Country Stamps

DURING THE 1950S THERE WERE SEVERAL CALLS TO ISSUE MORE PICTORIAL DEFINITIVE STAMPS. The feelings being expressed were that stamps could be far more effective in reflecting the heritage and scenery of the United Kingdom. The problem then, and still remains true today, is that including too much in a stamp design results in a cluttered appearance that destroys the dignity demanded of a definitive. Increasing the size of the definitives would not find favour with most users, who prefer the size of the stamps as they have presently evolved.

However, one solution did emerge from the discussions. This was the issue of distinctive stamps for the regions of the United Kingdom. In 1958 distinctive definitives were produced for Guernsey, Isle of Man, Jersey, Northern Ireland, Scotland and Wales. In the case of the three 'islands', just a 3d value was issued, while in the other three cases the values were 3d, 6d and 1s 3d. These stamps were primarily sold and used in the respective areas, although they were valid for postage throughout the United Kingdom.

The designs included the Dorothy Wilding Studio portrait of the Queen, denomination and symbols to represent the regions, but no inscriptions. Later, 2½d values were added for the Channel Islands and Isle of Man for use on postcards. Changes in postal rates necessitated the addition of 4d and 5d values for all regions, and also of 9d and 1s 6d values for Northern Ireland, Scotland and Wales.

In 1969 the constitution of the Post Office (the term Royal Mail was not generally used until 1986) was changed – it became a public corporation – and, as a consequence, the Channel Islands and Isle of Man were permitted to run their own independent postal administrations. Guernsey and Jersey took up the option from the outset, releasing their own stamps on 1 October 1969. From that date, United Kingdom stamps, including both the standard definitives and 'regional' issues, ceased to be sold over post office counters on the islands. The Isle of Man did not take up the option until 1973.

ISSUED STAMPS FOR
SCOTLAND, *1958.*

ISSUED STAMP FOR
JERSEY, *1958.*

ISSUED STAMPS FOR
NORTHERN IRELAND,
1958.

ISSUED STAMP FOR
ISLE OF MAN, *1958.*

ISSUED STAMPS FOR
WALES, *1958.*

ISSUED STAMP FOR
GUERNSEY, *1958.*

MACHIN VERSIONS *for
Scotland, Northern Ireland
and Wales stamps, 1971.*

MACHIN VERSION *for an
Isle of Man stamp, 1971.*

THIS UNUSUAL LETTER
BOX *can be found on the
Isle of Arran .*

FIRST DAY COVERS,
PRESENTATION PACKS AND
PRESTIGE STAMP BOOKS *relating to*
Scotland, Wales and Northern Ireland
are all collectable items.

ROYAL MAIL
DEFINITIVE
STAMPS

SCOTLAND

WALES

NORTHERN IRELAND

Mrs J Robinson
200 Manorbier Road
ILKESTON

Mrs J Robinson
200 Manorbier Road

Portmeirion, y pentref
Eiddolaidd a grewyd gan
Clough Williams-Ellis.

Portmeirion, the baroque
village created by Clough
Williams-Ellis.

Arweithtu o ymwelwyr i
chwareli Llechwedd a
Gloddfa Ganol 25,
Amgueddfa Werin Cymru
yn Sain Ffagan 26 a
Chanolfan y Dechnoleg
Amgen ym Machynlleth
27. Mae Gŵyl Gerddi
Cymru Glynebwy '92 28,
ar agor o fis Mai hyd fis
Hydref.

Popular with visitors are
the slate quarries of
Llechwedd and Gloddfa
Ganol 25, the Welsh Folk
Museum at St Fagans 26
and the Centre for
Alternative Technology at
Machynlleth 27. The
Garden Festival Wales
Ebbw Vale '92 28, is open
from May to October.

Garden Festival Wales
Gŵyl Gerddi Cymru
Ebbw Vale 92

The Scots were great explorers and
inventors. Kirkpatrick MacMillan
(1813-78), invented the bicycle.
Top (left to right), Sir Alexander Fleming
(1881-1955), discovered penicillin; Alexander
Graham Bell (1847-1922), invented the telephone;
John Napier (1550-1617), created logarithms;
James Clerk Maxwell (1831-79), made discoveries
in electricity and magnetism. Centre (left to right),
James Young Simpson (1811-70),
discovered chloroform; Sir Robert
Watson-Watt (1892-1973), developed
the use of radar; Sir John Ross
(1777-1856), traversed Baffin Bay;
James Watt (1736-1819), devised the
separate condenser for the steam engine.
Below (left to right), David Livingstone
(1813-73), missionary in Central
Africa; John Logie Baird (1888-1946),
pioneered television; Sir William
Jardine (1784-1843) and James
Matheson (1796-1878), established a
trading post in Hong Kong;
John Loudon McAdam (1756-1836),
(silhouette), roadbuilder and James
Young (1811-83), manufacturer of paraffin wax
and founder of the
mineral oil industry.

THE EIGHTEENTH CENTURY AND THE DAWN of
the nineteenth century witnessed a great
explosion of art and enlightenment. Artists,
thinkers, architects and writers spread their influence far
beyond the boundaries of Scotland.

Above; Sir Walter Scott (1771-1832), whose
novels inspired a sense of history and identity.
Above left; Robert Burns (1759-96), a farmer's
son who became Scotland's national poet.
Below left; Adam Smith (1723-90), author of
An Inquiry into the Nature and Causes
of the Wealth of Nations.

The introduction of decimal currency saw the need to provide new definitives specifically for the 'regions' (now excluding the Channel Islands). Clearly the Machin portrait would now need to be used, and indeed it would be sensible to mirror the design of the standard Machin definitives.

Jeffery Matthews provided the solution, by slightly reducing the size of the portrait and including suitable symbols in the top left-hand corner of each stamp. For each region, a common design was used for each denomination. For the Isle of Man the symbol chosen was the Three Legs of Man; for Northern Ireland, the Red Hand of Ulster; for Scotland, the Scottish Lion; and for Wales, the Dragon.

For each area, four values were produced – 2½p; 3p; 5p and 7½p. As before, these were primarily sold and used in the specific regional areas, but they were valid throughout the United Kingdom.

On 5 July 1973 the Isle of Man accepted postal independence and started to issue its own stamps, so no further 'regional' stamps were produced for the island. However, specific stamps for the key postal rates continue in use for Northern Ireland, Scotland and Wales: these are now designated as 'Country' stamps. As with the standard definitives, as postal rates have changed, so further values have been added to the range of Country definitives. However, such stamps normally appear a few weeks after any tariff change since there is no such urgency to provide currently valid denominations as there is with the standard definitives.

While at first these Country definitives were printed in photogravure by Harrison & Sons, they are now all printed in lithography by The House of Questa.

A POSTAL BUS *in Glencoe, West Scotland.*

A REGULAR DELIVERY *in Builth Wells, Wales.*

ROYAL MAIL *delivery to a distillery in Northern Ireland.*

Collectable

FIRST DAY COVERS ARE THE BEST KNOWN OF ALL THE COLLECTABLE ITEMS LINKED WITH STAMPS. These pictorial envelopes have a design linked to an issue of stamps, which are affixed to the envelope and cancelled on their first day of issue, often with a specially designed postmark.

However, it was not until the early 1960s that the need for special facilities for stamp collectors was accepted, and arrangements were made for those wishing to prepare first

FIRST DAY COVER
AND PRESENTATION
PACK *for issues of
definitive stamps.*

day covers. Previously collectors had had to make their own arrangements for preparing these covers, and thus it is not always easy to find covers for definitives stamps issued up to the early years of the reign of Elizabeth II. The difficulties encountered by collectors were not helped by the fact that in those days advance notice of new stamp issues was not always forthcoming, and, particularly in the case of definitives, not all post offices received stocks of a new issue on its first day of release.

This did not prevent first day covers existing, of course, indeed even of the Penny Black – although clearly the senders did not in all probability realise they were producing such historic and collectable documents. The Penny Black was put on sale on 1 May 1840, but it was not officially intended for use until five days later, on 6 May. Examples of usage are known dated 6 May, but the earliest recorded use is in fact 2 May 1840. A cover bearing a Penny Black dated 2 May 1840 was auctioned in 1991 and fetched more than $2.4 million.

By the time the Machin definitives were released in 1967, Royal Mail had fully recognised the existence of collectors, and was providing full first day cover facilities each time new values were added to the range. These facilities included specially designed envelopes as well as posting boxes at main post offices for the stamps and covers to receive a special handstamp reading First Day of Issue.

On the introduction of decimal currency on 15 February 1971, the intention was to provide the same service. Unfortunately these plans were thwarted by a strike, which meant that a nationwide collection and delivery service was not possible. However, first day covers posted in the special boxes provided after the conclusion of the strike in March of that year, were duly handstamped with the date the decimal definitives were officially issued. These covers also bear a legend identifying them as having been delayed by the strike. Support for the strike was not total, however, and in many areas postal services functioned as normal. It is thus possible to find covers posted and delivered locally genuinely cancelled on 15 February, although these tend to bear normal post office cancellations rather than a First Day of Issue special handstamp.

Full first day cover facilities continue to be provided whenever there are significant changes to the definitive range, such as a change of colour or new denominations. Naturally such changes include the release of high value definitives and new Country definitives. Sometimes, for operational reasons, other changes occur that are noted by specialist collectors. However, they often pass unnoticed by the majority of collectors and so are not necessarily afforded a first day of issue service.

Where such a service is provided, a pictorial envelope is offered and, in addition to First Day of Issue handstamps at a large number of centres, Royal Mail also provides special cancellations at two locations. These are generally at Windsor Post Office and at the British Philatelic Bureau in Edinburgh, where pictorial cancellations are designed to complement the stamps perfectly.

At the same time as special services for collectors were being introduced, a new item was conceived – the presentation pack. These packs contain a new set of stamps, slipped into a black protective card, and surrounded by a folder giving background information about the issue. The whole is encased in a clear wrapping.

Packs were also produced in 1960 containing all of the then current definitives, low and high value, and the various 'regionals'. These came in two forms, for sale in the United Kingdom and also for sale in the USA.

Once all of the low values of the Machin definitives had been released in 1968, a presentation pack was produced containing one of each value. Likewise, on the introduction of decimal currency, a pack was produced containing one of each value as originally released. The low value presentation pack is revised from time to time as changes in denominations make a new pack necessary.

For the Country definitives, packs were provided for the pre-decimal values from each of Northern Ireland, Scotland and Wales, and for the same regions plus the Isle of Man containing the initial four values released after the introduction of decimal currency. Subsequently the packs for Northern Ireland, Scotland and Wales were amended as changes to the range of definitive values dictated. Likewise presentation packs were provided for the high value definitives, starting with the Machin series of 1969. For the Machin high values printed in photogravure, a pack was produced for the initial three values (£1, £2 and £5) and subsequently for the £1.60 'parcel' value added in 1987, but not for any of the intervening 'parcel' stamps.

An item introduced in 1973 that has grown in popularity is the 'stamp card', originally known as the PHQ (Postal Headquarters) card. Such cards feature an enlarged version of a stamp design, and now accompany each special issue. They have generally not been produced in conjunction with the low value definitives, although included among the special postcards produced from time to time by the National Postal Museum have been cards reproducing the low value Machin definitive design. However, a stamp card was issued in conjunction with the release of the first-class self-adhesive stamp in October 1993. This stamp features a variation of the Machin design, in that it has a landscape (horizontal) format instead of the more usual portrait (vertical) one.

With the release of the £10 definitive on 2 March 1993, a stamp card was produced of this impressive stamp design. However, to maintain the security of the stamp, a number of subtle changes differentiate the actual stamp from the design featured on the card. Some time can be spent on a 'spot the differences' quest. Although the actual stamps had been issued some twelve months earlier, stamp cards were at the same time issued featuring the designs of the four Castle high values with the security features such as elliptical perforations.

Definitives offer collectors a great deal of choice. A collection can be as straightforward or as specialised as the collector personally determines. The brilliance of the designs is evidenced by the fact that they remain in use for many years, and look as fresh as when first conceived. They provide an ever-growing collection, one that requires nothing more than a periodic visit to a post office to keep it up to date.

A CROWN OPTICAL GLASS PYRAMID *incorporating a mint £1 stamp.*

Glossary

Country stamps	from 1973 stamps issued for Scotland, Northern Ireland and Wales.
definitive	stamp on long term sale, not issued for any special occasion.
embossing	method of printing used especially for some Victorian stamps, with the design in white standing proud of the surface.
essays	trial stamps, of design or colour, not issued to the public.
first day cover	envelope, usually pictorial, with stamps used on the first day of issue.
graphite	black lines of Naphthadag applied on the back of Wilding definitives in 1957-59 to assist the ALF facing and cancelling machines.
gravure	see photogravure.
intaglio	method of printing, also called recess or line engraving, where the stamp is printed from a recessed image, and the ink stands proud of the surface, used for the Penny Black etc, and most high values.
letterpress	method of printing, also called surface or relief printing, where stamps are printed from images with a raised surface which impress on the paper, used for later Victorian stamps and up to 1934 (with one later issue).
litho(graphy)	method of printing in which ink is applied selectively to the plate by chemically treating image areas to accept ink and non-image areas to accept water.
Machins	definitives designed by Arnold Machin from his plaster cast of Queen Elizabeth II, in use from 1967.
Maltese Cross	first cancellation of postage stamps.
miniature sheet	small sheet in one overall design incorporating one or more stamps.
Non Value Indicator	(NVI) stamps without denomination but with 1st or 2nd class, remaining valid despite changes in tariff.
pane	the format of a number of stamps printed together, as in booklet pane or a sheet with two panes separated by a gutter margin.
perforation	holes round the margins of stamps to enable separation.
phosphor	agent printed in bands or in the paper coating of stamps to assist facing and cancelling, first used in 1959.
photogravure	method of printing in which recesses on a cylinder are filled with ink and the surplus removed with a blade, used for most British stamps since 1934.
PHQ card	postcard showing the enlarged stamp image (now termed Stamp card).
presentation pack	pack containing a set of stamps and an explanatory card.
recess	see intaglio.
Regionals	definitives issued for Scotland, Northern Ireland, Wales, Guernsey, Jersey and the Isle of Man from 1958. Later termed Country stamps.
Seahorse	design of the George V high value definitives.
stamp book(let)	pane(s) of stamps with margin, sold within outer covers.
stamp card	see PHQ card.
watermark	security device in the paper used from the Penny Black until discontinued in 1967.
Wilding	definitives issued from 1952 till 1967 using the portrait of Queen Elizabeth II taken by the Dorothy Wilding Studio.

PICTURE ACKNOWLEDGEMENTS

NPM: National Postal Museum. *PRD:* The Post Office Public Relations Department Photographic Library. ©*RM:* copyright Royal Mail
* Photographs taken by Rod Tidnam.

Pages 6 & 7 - *PRD*; pages 8 & 9 stamps - *NPM, others - PRD; pages 10 & 11 - PRD; pages 12 & 13 - NPM (*stamps); page 14 - PRD; pages 15, 16 & 17 - *NPM; pages 18 & 19 "retouching" - PRD, stamps - *NPM; page 20 - *NPM; pages 21, 22 & 23 - PRD; pages 24 & 25 - *NPM; pages 26 & 27 stamps - *NPM, others - PRD; pages 28 & 29 - *©RM; page 30 - *NPM; page 31 - *to come; page 33 - PRD; page 34 - *NPM; page 36 stamp - NPM, others - PRD; pages 37 & 38 - *NPM; page 39 notice - NPM, photo - PRD; pages 40 & 41 - PRD; page 42 sale of stamps - PRD, others - *©RM; page 43 advertisements - NPM, photo - PRD; pages 44 & 45 stamps - *NPM, photos - PRD; pages 46 & 47 NPM, pages 48 & 49 stamps *NPM, photo - PRD; page 50 - *©RM; page 51 - PRD; pages 52 & 54 - *©RM.